Issue Three

Bringing together the latest science with powerful narratives, *Any Last Words?* was founded with the belief that emotivity and creativity will help people understand and engage with the implications of our changing climate.

This collection was submitted by a variety of young authors from across the United Kingdom, shortlisted for this anthology by both scientists and creative writers working at the University of East Anglia (UEA) for your pleasure, and attention.

This is the third edition of the *Any Last Words?* anthology. Issue #1 and #2 are available for purchase from www.eggboxpublishing.com

Read on if you dare.

Any Last Words?

First published in 2020 by Eggbox, an imprint
of UEA Publishing Project.

*UEA Publishing Project, Office MUS1.02, Interdisciplinary Institute
for the Humanities, University of East Anglia, Norwich, NR4 7TJ.*

Design and Illustration by Michaela-Jay Appleton
Project Administration by Connor Enright

All rights reserved.

*Every effort has been made to obtain the necessary permissions
with reference to copyright material both illustrative and quoted.
We apologise for any acknowledgements in any future edition.*

Issue Three

The collation of this anthology is dedicated to those scientists, authors and artists inspiring a thirst for knowledge and understanding in our society.

Curiosity makes children of us all.

−

Content Warning:

This anthology tackles distressing themes of climate breakdown which may be upsetting to some readers.

For those readers struggling with climate anxiety, we recommend the resources of the Climate Psychology Alliance; available via www.climatepsychologyalliance.org

Any Last Words?

Issue Three

Contents

2	A Letter From My Mother	*Chloe Yates*
5	Bear With	*Marnie Cavill*
6	Deadline	*Oliver Shrouder*
9	Eden Orchard	*Elsy Leslie*
		Long Form Winner
15	Epitaph	*Alice Avery*
16	Futility in Sustainability	*Marnie Cavill*
17	Knitting	*Chloe Yates*
		Short Form Winner
18	Last Night I Bought Some Oreos	*Dana Elizabeth*
19	Melt	*Alex Howe*
20	Sticking It	*Alex Curry*
		Grand Prize Winner

Any Last Words?

Issue Three

Acknowledgements

We are not a large project, but with the support and guidance of the following, we act beyond our own limitations.

A huge thank you to Jemma Williams, Meg Watts, Ryan Lenney and all of the extended *Any Last Words?* team for their editorial support, scientific moderation and all-round assistance in making this project a reality. We would also like to recognise the numerous UEA staff who have helped judging, promoting and supporting this project and the authors within.

Conversations with the following contributors provided invaluable guidance and inspiration throughout the production of this issue:

Dr Tom Hargreaves – School of Environmental Sciences, UEA
Nathan Hamilton – BoilerHouse Press
Emma Seager, Clea Licht & Elizabeth Yew – EggBox Publishing

The *Any Last Words?* project was realised with the financial support of our sponsors, SustainSuccess Ltd, who have continued to contribute to environmental, community and social projects as part of their mission to fight the climate crisis and improve our world for all. You can find out more by visiting:
www.sustainsuccess.co.uk

Finally, thank you to those who have purchased this anthology, followed the project or chose to submit works, the journey is not over and we need your passion now more than ever.

A Letter From My Mother

Chloe Yates

Dear Chloe,

Hello, little one. This is your mother Gaia writing. I know that you're a grown woman now and you like to think you're independent. But I wanted to send you this letter anyway. Because a mother's instincts are strong and I can see when any of my children are hurting.

I see how much grief you are carrying, and fear, and anger. It looks heavy. And hot. But I can also see its roots. Roots of plants often look very different to the plants themselves, don't they, and the mycelial network looks completely different to the mushrooms. Roots look different. And your grief that feels too heavy, your anger that burns through you like a forest fire, these are rooted in love. Remember that.

Thank you for taking to the streets. For taking that drum of yours and marching through worlds of concrete and power and beating it until your hands bleed, I can hear you. I can hear all of you. Marching for me. Singing for me. But now, listen to me, and this is very important. You mustn't let this anger overcome you. Roots need water, food. They need to be fed if the plant is to flourish. And as your mother, I must remind you to feed yourself.

So spend time in my fragile, precious woods. Let my trees hold you, let my rivers sing to you.

Spend time gazing at the vastness of my sky. See how it never stays the same for too long.

Spend time with my squirrels. See how they leap fearlessly from branch to branch, trusting they will land.

Spend time with the brambles, and the nettles. See how there is beauty in chaos.

Spend time with my mushrooms. See how there is life, even in death.

Spend time with my oceans. See how power is not all about money.

Spend time lying curled up in my grass. Remember that I held you as you took your first breath, and I will hold you when you take your last.

And then, when you feel like your roots are full to bursting, pick yourself up, and walk gently back upon my soil.

This is a very powerful time, child. There is lots to do and not much time to do it in. But when times are urgent, slow down. When times are urgent, slow down. When times. Are urgent. Slow. Down. I am okay, you see. I am hurting, but I am okay.

Any Last Words?

I am not afraid, of what is to come. You do not need to be afraid either. Fear is paralysing. Do what you can, but release the things you cannot control.

Okay. I have harked on at you enough. I know you're a grown woman now. I know you like to think you're independent. But I am always here, my love. Any time you want to chat. Remember that I am always here.

Infinite love,
Your Mother Gaia.

Bear With

Marnie Cavill

Our food is full of chemicals,
Processed, like the people at our borders.
Ocean levels are rising
Somewhere, a seagull drips in tar
The planet is heating up,
Much like our political climate.
More and more women die every day from violent attacks
Daughters, sisters, mothers.
We are a species cut up.

And the government does nothing.
Because we are young
And don't know any better.

Deadline

Oliver Shrouder

I remember the comfort of the *good old days*
when we were told we had until 2040
to save the planet, the *good old days*
when we had twelve years to go
without the worry of change, the terror
of choosing vegetable sausages
with our Full English, white-bread
sandwiches with just cucumber,
when we still had our plastic straws
our Tesco pasta pots our coffee cups
our single use carrier bags
which we happily black-binned;
the *good old days* when that dark portal
took our waste to the infinite not-here,
where dumps were so far from city centres
that even the smell was no concern:
all we had to smell was breath, air freshener –
these are now the *good old days*.

Now we have eighteen months –
eighteen months
to panic in our apartments
with no room or lease
for composting,

eighteen months to undo the shame of fast fashion
discovering gelatin
in the already bought packet of chews
discovering gelatin
in the already bought iron supplements
and the discovery of dread
on every restaurant menu
eighteen months in which to pot plants the corners
of our plastic Ikea furniture
and hope this is enough to purify the air,
eighteen months to watch the politicians we did not vote for

Any Last Words?

fly to climate conferences in private jets
and suits they will never wear again
sourced sustainably
by the calloused and underpaid
eighteen months to politicise our cartons of milk
and the almonds that forests died for
eighteen months to cancel our cards
refuse to pay our bills
and live aesthetically on wild berries
knowing that in a year
these eighteen months
will have been the *good old days*
these eighteen months
how free we were back then
knowing that in these eighteen months
our choices have changed
a percentage of a percentage
of the 71%
caused by the people
we can't afford to read about
and can't afford to meet.

Eden Orchard

Long Form Winner

Elsy Leslie

So it starts—again—in a garden. The groundsman is here year-round, six days a week, sunrise to sunset, but you wouldn't think so looking at it. You wouldn't think so looking at him, either, wheezing as he negotiates your way through the thicket. When the thorns snag his coat he doesn't notice until they pull, and then he thumps them off with the nonstrategic fervour of a man who has never set foot off concrete.

You're not having a much easier time of it. Even vaulting the grass is a struggle now: at the perimeter it lay flat on the tarmac like a pod of beached whales, but here the tallest stalks brush the backs of his thighs and the shorter ones scrub your ankles like stakes. There's no pattern to their placement, either; just the happenstance of their breeding, with ugly white flowers dotting the floor like mould. They form a furious patchwork of microscopic order that you needn't bother attending to.

Sure, it often starts in a garden. What you have to realise is that a garden makes for a rather efficient starting point. Gardens like this one, almost nothing imposed on it except the word you chose as you entered: *garden*. The whole place stutters like an engine on the verge of combustion, something always undulating beneath your feet, chirping at the back of your ear, but don't turn around, don't look at what's behind you. It's starting in a garden.

"Is there something you could do about this?" You won't say, but you're tormented by the thought of sap and insect blood on your new boots.

The old man laughs, though he barely has the breath to, raises his knee over a thick mound of grass and stomps. It hurls him off within the second. The strands flicker delicately at their full height, creases smoothed and almost invisible. The groundsman regains his balance and presses on. You follow.

"Just thought it'd make your commute easier," you mutter. He must live close by. Surely not on the premises. He doesn't pay rent.

"We're almost there."

When you reach the orchard, the world grows a little tamer. You suppose the trees suckle up most of the rain. The ground is a little easier to traverse, but it's all you can do not to stop at every tree and wonder if this is the tree, The Tree—search its trunk for a burn scar, or something, coiled around like a rope, search the groundsman's face for a flash of unease or quiet recognition. But each scrawl of bark is as unreadable as the last and if he ever turns around it's to look at you, blankly, checking for further orders.

"Seems alright," you say. You look up. The fruits swim in the air like sluggish pendulums, straining arcs into their branches. "What's the delay?" You reach up to tug one from its socket. At first, it resists.

Issue Three

"They won't be ripe for another month or so," the groundsman says. You heave with all your weight until the fruit finally comes unstuck—pop—and the branch ricochets, sets the whole tree rattling. The groundsman watches. He seems unimpressed.

It doesn't *look* unripe until you take a bite and the flesh crumbles in your mouth like lukewarm ice. It doesn't taste of much more than ice, either, until the delayed, dangerously subtle taste of sour milk or rotten eggs. The groundsman turns around as you empty your mouth against the tree trunk.

"A month, was it?"

"Thereabouts."

You spit again. "That's too long. We've had such a good first year—we can't afford to run out now." The groundsman shrugs disaffectedly. "What would it cost to plant another orchard for a year-round supply?"

"Can't be done." His voice is gruff, hard with resentment. You're not sure if it's for you or the trees. "They don't grow a few miles outside the garden, let alone the other side of the world."

"So plant them near the garden."

He parts his lips. They hover around each other for a moment before settling into an uneasy, open smile. "And get them to yield in the middle of winter?"

Why not? You don't ask, but his face goes soft with recognition.

"They won't flower outside of spring. If you wanted a year-round yield, you'd have to farm internationally, or–" He winces in consideration. "There's always controlled environments. Greenhouses."

You spin to face the garden. You want to shake it off, that look of understanding, sympathy he's giving you. It feels invasive, almost, like fingers drifting through your skin and bristling your guts. The taste of stillborn fruit is still heavy on your tongue.

"There's always town," he says.

People live in the town, though. You don't think that's worth pointing out, because not only does he know, he knows you're thinking it. "Would it be impossible just to build in the garden?"

"Not impossible," he says gently. "Just hard."

Expensive, that means. "What about the people?" you ask. He raises his hands in surrender, exorcising himself from the situation. It's not up to him.

Up to you, you suppose: you and the shareholders and the rest of the Board. You weigh up the costs in your mind, strike them down, race through different hypotheticals. Buying out rental properties. Displacing a town. How far would that set you back? Not too far, monetarily speaking, but it gets more complicated when you take into consideration the potential for public backlash. With a year-round output, though, a permanent chokehold on the market—

PR would hardly be a consideration.

You collect yourself when you remember the groundsman, but he—thank god—is stumbling away amongst the trees, his back to you. It's not a decision that needs to be made yet, you think. Just a decision you might never, ever come back from.

You swallow.

Epitaph

Alice Avery

Contrails,
clouds
the path isn't quite as clear
does the journey matter?
Isn't it the destination that counts
Not how we got there

tossing money spiders
over our shoulders
into metal water
if this can survive a few
thousand years,
fed by virgins,
why can't our mum's house?

Why can't the garden we grew,
chose the purple pansies
with the orange roses
Why can't they last a bit longer?
We tried

to stay awake at least
and to clear the air of lice
with a less efficient
nit comb, not like
the one still on mum's bathroom shelf
dusty and rusted
not fine-toothed enough to clear
dioxin from the river
the one that gives us eczema flare ups,
puts these sheets of promises in our hands.
Telling us all the good news.

Phasing down
1.5c
2030

Mum always said numbers were a cop a shit.
Guess there wasn't enough blood in the soil
to last this long. The fuel ran out.

We'll try.

Futility in Sustainability

Marnie Cavill

Terry Pratchett once said something about how a man
who could afford fifty-dollar boots would have dry feet
for 10 years.
But a poor man who could only afford cheap boots
would spend a hundred dollars in the same amount
of time,
And would still have wet feet.

Being sustainable has the same principle,
Sometimes disposable is all someone can afford.
But we cannot afford for our planet to become disposable.

The rich blame the poor,
When the poor have no power,
And live in a society structured by the rich.

It is all our fault.

Knitting

Short Form Winner

Chloe Yates

I sit and knit at the feet of the police
Knit songs and drums and rallying cries
into these gloves I make, preparing for winter.
I knit the stories that surround me,
the laughing women with weather beaten skin,
fire in their eyes, talking about Greenham
and the mud! oh remember the mud!
Knit one purl one, I knit the stony boredom
of the police, I knit the beat of the drums,
catch the heartbeat of the rebellion
with my needle and I knit one, purl one.
I catch the cry of the woman behind me
glued high up for all of Oxford Circus to see.
She calls for water?! Can I get some water?!
Someone feeds her water, rubs sun cream
onto her sun-kissed face and the neon circle
tightens around our necks. Still we sing.
Still I knit. Still the stories flow.
The sun starts to lower and the black boots twitch.
We will stay for as long as it takes in this too-hot heat.
And I will knit my gloves, for they will keep me warm in winter.
I'm trying to think ahead, you see.

Last Night I Bought Some Oreos

Dana Elizabeth

Gaia, forgive me. They looked like pop art amongst the clinical white of Tesco. They were double stuffed and I've inherited nothing if not Dad's sweet tooth. I binged on them -- chocolate junkie, saturated with fat -- and binned the plastic wrapper. Gaia, my speckled teeth became oozing bog-thick tear tracks like a cavern in each cheek. Greed subsided, gave way to a palm oil hangover that only hair of the dog could fix. I bought another pack because every addict knows how terrifying it is to become acclimatised. Then, Gaia, I counted the cookies, equated it to damage I had done. Plush orangutan pelts now slick, brown and red on the rainforest floor. How perverse, that I could care for you so much and kill you for so little. My mindless sweet tooth wants to slaughter your sweet babies. Gaia, why does your sickness feel to me like it came from a dirty needle I plunged through your skin? Why do I call it your sickness? I wish I could scrub your mossy blood off of my hangman's hands without wasting another single-use baby wipe.

Melt

Alex Howe

Paper scraps start to ignite, and she tells me this tongue is a clipper
when I know if I could choose I'd at least be matches.
She complains that the smell of crisp koalas above
has infiltrated her hair.
The water is creeping between our toes, but sure
let's talk about my propensity for skimming stones
and the tsunamis it creates.
I never did keep all my bottle tops.
Soon, we will sink into the mud, and you'll tell me it's my fault
it isn't sunny, so we can't crack our way out of split earth.
When the snowstorms start,
I promise I'll keep wearing the flip flops you bought me,
and turn crystal into stone. I'll call the ground shaking a lullaby.
The cliffs will crumble and I'll catch the debris in a plastic bag
for you to bandage back on.
I'll find the fuzzy body of the last bee on the pavement,
and hide the corpse –
so you don't accuse me of having killed him.
I'll be the best dressed guest at his funeral.
I'll carve my feelings out of ice and float them across warm water.
I will feign surprise when they disappear.

Sticking It

Grand Prize Winner

Alex Curry

A busy walkway around the UEA campus
Jamie (J) and **Charlie (C)** enter. Perhaps they lay out a mat/carpet with a road painted on it, perhaps not. Either way, they lie down on the floor
They should interact with the surrounding people in a lighthearted and comedic manner (maybe throw in an "I'm lying here" as someone steps over them particularly ungraciously), feel free to use lines from the script, but I reckon most people will just ignore them (it's Britain after all). Someone may engage and ask what they're doing, in which case use the script to improvise an in character response

Scene
If nobody elects to interact, run this scene
J   Why here?
C   Pardon?
J   Why this road?
C   It's busy.
J   I haven't seen a single car.
C   There's foot traffic.
J   Who can simply step over us.
C   And?
J   Well a car can't do that. They'd have to stop. Or kill us.

C They wouldn't do that.
J I wouldn't be so sure.
C Come off it.
J I'm serious. You know Margaret? A soccer mum in a SUV nearly did her in last week. A Range Rover. That'd be a terrible way to go.
C Hit by a car?
J Hit by a <u>Range Rover.</u>
C Oh. Yeah. Anyway, this is a good spot. Foot traffic is good.
J In what way?
C Easier to interact with, motorists just get pissed. Watch this: *(to passerby* Hey, you. Yeah, you! How you doing? (response) Oh yeah, same, thank you. (to **J**) See, easy.
J What was that?
C A happy interaction.
J A pointless interaction.
C No.
J Yes! The whole reason we block roads is because it gets headlines. Generates attention, press, then people go check out our website, learn about the cause. If you're gonna target foot traffic, you've gotta do it like this: *(to passerby)* Do you have a minute to talk about the climate emergency?
        *(If ignored/non-committal response,
        continue. If engaged, skip to mark)*
No? That's okay, thank you!
C That was just as useless.

J At least they know we're doing this for a reason, you basically just said hi. If they'd wanted to talk, I would have tried the sell.
C Alrighty, what does the "sell" sound like then?

(If engaged, start here)

J How do you sleep at night? Well? Warmly? Not for too much longer you won't. In our last "normal" winter, 8,500 lives were lost as a result of cold or leaky homes. Sickness associated with poor housing costs the NHS £2.5 billion every year. This will only get worse as the impacts of climate change increase, which is why Insulate Britain is demanding government action now, to prevent a national catastrophe in the future.
C Jesus Christ.
J What?
C That was hostile, aggressive, ineffectual scare mongering.
J People should be scared.
C Maybe, but that doesn't mean it's a good point of engagement. You've gotta give people a bit of hope, show them there's something they can do.
J Go on.
C You're probably wondering why I'm lying on this road here. Well, we are doing this to get the attention of the government. Insulate Britain demands that the UK government immediately promises to full

fund and take responsibility for the insulation of all social housing in Britain by 2025 and produces, within four months, a legally binding national plan for a low energy, low carbon retrofit of all homes by 2030.

J That was from the website.
C And?
J You can't just quote the website at people.
C Why not? It's designed to put across our message. To sell the cause.
J The website is general, it's aim is to cater to anyone, market to everyone. Here, on the road, you gotta make it personal.
C You're impossible.
J I'm trying to help. We've gotta work together.
C Your approach is ridiculous.
J You know, I don't have to deal with this. I'm off to sit on an actual road. Maybe I'll get killed by a Range Rover. Generate some headlines.
C But we're glued down, we can't move.
J *stands up*
    Wha-? Huh?
J *walks off*
    I'm glued down! Jamie! Jamie!
Silence
    Twat.

Charlie lies alone for a bit, interacts with a few more people, before peeling themselves up, taking the mat, and leaving

The Project Moving Forward

The imagining of new futures, and the reconciliation of science and society are ongoing processes. The climatic change we all face will not only continue, but accelerate, and our actions now matter more than ever in mitigating this crisis. Adapting to our futures, whatever they may be will require more than just the technical fields; engaging and integrating of artists and publics around the world will be essential for generating new meanings and means of survival.

We encourage you to keep reading; both the stories and the science emerging from our changing world.

We implore you to keep asking; the questions that matter to you as individuals, and for your institutions to mitigate and adapt to the climatic changes threatening all our cares.

We hope that you will keep imagining; not just the uncertain times that lay ahead, but where we can find opportunities in the coming change, to better care for each other and the world we live in.

We at *Any Last Words?* will keep working.

The story isn't over yet.

Resources

This project does not stand alone but as part of wider communities of science, communication and co-production uniting scientists and the public in creating knowledge, understanding and a brighter future. In recognition of this, we would like to promote the valuable work of related institutions and projects below:

The *Tyndall Centre* is working from campuses at UEA and across the UK to "undertake robust and independent research to identify the challenges and opportunities presented by climate change, and inform open and transparent decisions that best serve society": tyndall.ac.uk

For those wishing to explore poets responding to the climate crisis, we would recommend *Magma 72: the Climate Change Issue:* magmapoetry.com/archive/magma-72

For those interested in the University of East Anglia's co-production community we suggest you explore the work of the *Science, Society and Sustainability* (3S) research group: 3Sresearch.org

www.ingramcontent.com/pod-product-compliance
Ingram Content Group UK Ltd.
Pitfield, Milton Keynes, MK11 3LW, UK
UKHW021907220225
455423UK00011B/91